# REPTILES OF THE WORLD FUN FACTS FOR KIDS

**BABY PROFESSOR**

EDUCATION KIDS

Speedy Publishing LLC
40 E. Main St. #1156
Newark, DE 19711
www.speedypublishing.com

Reptiles are a group
of animals comprising
today's turtles,
crocodilians, snakes,
lizards, tuatara, and their
extinct relatives.

There are more than
8,000 species of
reptiles on the planet.
Reptiles are among
the longest-lived
species on the planet.

Reptiles are covered
in scales or have
a bony external
plate such as a
shell. Reptiles do
not have sweat or
sebaceous glands.

Chameleons do not change their color to blend in with different backgrounds; the color change is due to temperature or humidity and emotions, such as anger and fear.

Reptiles are cold-blooded animals, which means that they depend on external sources to maintain their body temperatures.

Reptiles are thought
to have evolved
about 340 million
years ago from a
group of reptile-like
amphibians called
the Reptiliomorphs.

Reptiles are tetrapods which means they have 4 limbs. Although snakes have lost their legs during the course of evolution, they are tetrapods by descent.

Reptiles can be found
on every continent
except for Antarctica.